Mom-Speak

Written by Rebecca Rock

new seasons™

*W*atch out,

or your FACE will **FREEZE** that way.

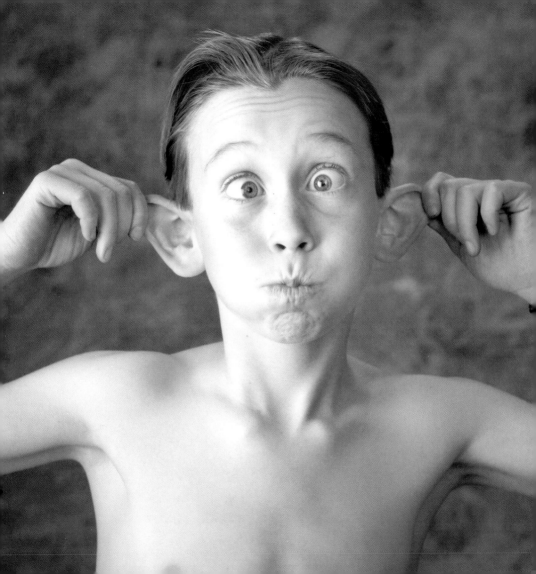

$\mathcal{D}$id you
WASH
BEHIND
your
EARS?

8

You'll **EAT** me out of HOUSE and HOME!

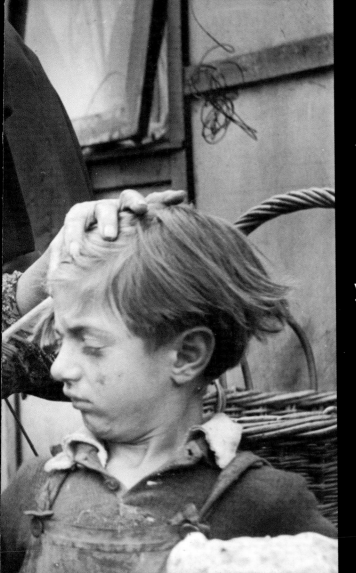

When was
the last time
you COMBED
your **HAIR**?

$\mathcal{D}$id you
MAKE your
BED yet?

$\mathcal{E}$at your BREAD CRUSTS.

It'll make your hair **CURLY.**

$\mathcal{A}$re you

LISTENING

to ME?

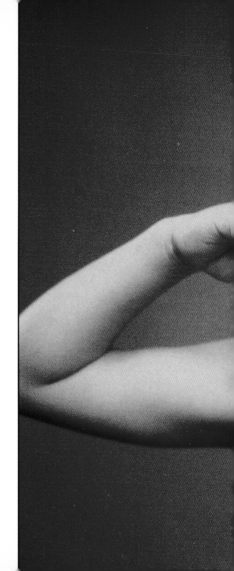

Don't **MAKE ME** come

in there. . . .

19

$\mathcal{D}$o **NOT** get
that dress
DIRTY!

20

$\mathcal{I}$ CAN'T LEAVE YOU alone

for a **MINUTE**!

*C*lean your plate or there's **NO DESSERT** for you.

Well . . . first tell me what's for dessert.

24

Sit up

straight!

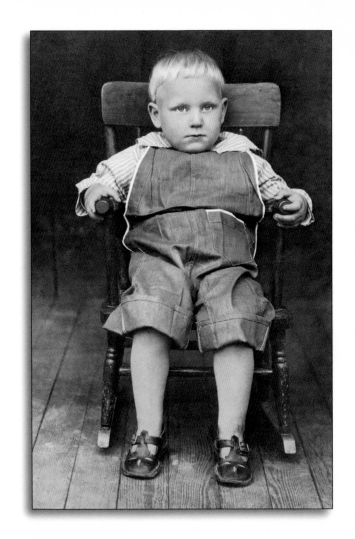

$\mathcal{I}$f your friends jumped off a **BRIDGE,**

would you FOLLOW them?

Don't sit **SO CLOSE** to the TV.

$\mathcal{B}$e **GOOD** for the babysitter.

*Y*ou are

NOT LEAVING

this house

UNLESS

you're wearing

clean ***UNDERWEAR.***

$\mathcal{I}$f I've told you ONCE,

I've told you a **THOUSAND** times…

How much is a thousand?

$\mathcal{B}$reakfast is the
MOST IMPORTANT
meal of the **DAY.**

*U*se your
INSIDE
VOICE!

$\mathcal{G}$et down
from there
this
INSTANT!

Put that tooth under your pillow—
maybe the TOOTH FAIRY will take it and
leave you a little **PRESENT.**

Dear kids,

While we're gone,

DON'T have any friends over,

DON'T spend all your time on the phone,

ONLY one hour of television a day,

TAKE A BATH every night,

and GO TO BED before 10:00.

HAVE FUN.

Love, Mom

$\mathcal{M}$oney

doesn't grow

on **TREES.**

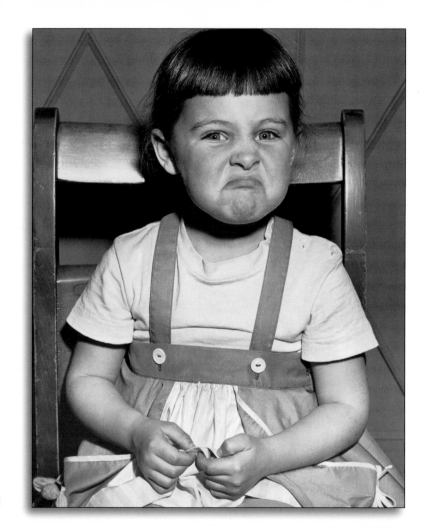

$\mathcal{I}$ think SOMEONE

needs a **TIME-OUT.**

$\mathcal{I}$f you eat too much CANDY,

your teeth will **ROT.**

$\mathcal{D}$rink your milk
so you'll grow up
BIG and **STRONG.**

*L*ook before

you leap.

*T*here's NO such word
as ***CAN'T.***

Don't **TALK** with your mouth full.

Stand still!

Do you have **ANTS** in your PANTS?

$\mathcal{B}$e **NICE** to your BROTHER.

$\mathcal{D}$on't cross your eyes—

they'll get **STUCK** that way.

The TELEPHONE is not a **TOY.**

Don't EAT that—

it'll give you **WORMS.**

No, you can't have a **SNACK.**

You'll SPOIL your APPETITE.

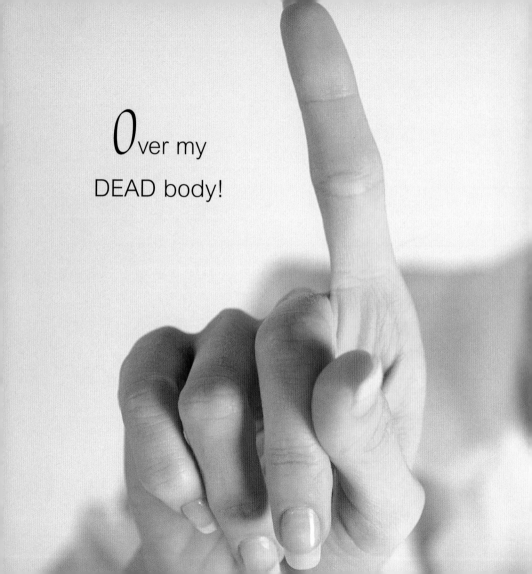

$\mathcal{E}$at your **VEGETABLES,** YOUNG LADY. It'll put hair on your chest.

You, young man, are getting TOO BIG for your BRITCHES!

$\mathcal{I}$f it didn't **TASTE BAD,**

it wouldn't be MEDICINE.

$\mathcal{R}$each for the **STARS.**

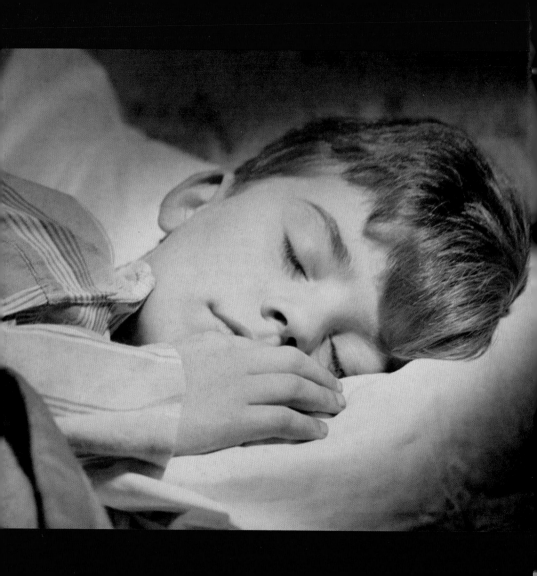

When I go to bed at night,

Mom tucks me in and holds me tight.

She kisses my cheek and

turns out the light,

Then stops at the door

to make sure I'm all right.

(Mostly I pretend I'm asleep.)